KRATOM MANUAL

An Extensive Look at Kratom's Various Functions, Reactions, and Other Features

DR. SIDWELL ELLIS

Table of Contents

CHAPTER ONE 3

KRATOM...3

An Extensive Look at Kratom's Various
Functions, Reactions, and Other Features.....3

Where does it come from, and why do people
use it?..6

CHAPTER TWO 10

Possibilities of inducing stimulation.............10

What about it causes debate? 12

Affects People Have Said They Feel 16

CHAPTER THREE...19

Methods and Primers 19

Can Kratom Help with Depression and
Anxiety? 21

CHAPTER FOUR 27

Additional Supposed Advantages 27

CHAPTER FIVE 35

Can you differentiate between varieties? ...35

CHAPTER ONE

KRATOM

An Extensive Look at Kratom's Various Functions, Reactions, and Other Features

When asked, "What is kratom?"

A member of the coffee family, the kratom tree (Mitragyna speciosa) grows in tropical climates. Its original range includes much of South Asia, including Thailand, Myanmar, and Malaysia.

Both stimulants and sedatives have been derived from the leaves. In addition to relieving opiate withdrawal symptoms, it has been reported to alleviate chronic pain and gastrointestinal issues.

However, sufficient clinical trials of kratom are lacking to fully understand its health effects.

The FDA has not yet green-lighted its use in medicine.

If you want to find out more about kratom, keep reading.

Is that allowed by the law?

In the USA, kratom has been legalized for use. Thailand, Australia, Malaysia, and a few other EU countries have outlawed the practice.

When sold in the United States, kratom is typically promoted as a complementary and alternative medicine. It's sold in health food and natural medicine shops.

It has been said that kratom can act as a stimulant in small doses. Low-dose users commonly report feeling more energized, alert, and social after taking the drug. According to some reports, kratom can be sedative at higher doses, leading to euphoric effects and a dampening of emotions and sensations.

The alkaloids mitragynine and 7-hydroxymitragynine are kratom's primary bioactive components. These alkaloids have been shown to have potential as analgesics (pain relievers), anti-inflammatory agents, and muscle relaxants. Consequently, kratom is frequently used to alleviate the pain and discomfort associated with fibromyalgia.

The dark green leaves of the plant are typically dried, crushed, or powdered. Powders of enhanced kratom exist, and they tend to be green or a light brown color. Other plant extracts are also included in these powders.

The herb can also be purchased in the form of a paste, capsule, or tablet. American consumers typically consume kratom in the

form of a tea to self-manage
pain and overcome opioid
withdrawal.

CHAPTER TWO

Possibilities of inducing stimulation

The European Monitoring Centre for Drugs and Drug Addiction (EMCDDA) reports that only a few grams is sufficient to produce stimulant effects. The peak of the effects occurs around 10 minutes after ingestion, and they can last for up to 1 1/2 hours. Many of the following effects are possible:

- alertness

- sociability

- giddiness

- impaired motor control

Influence on sedation

For a sedative effect, take 10–25 grams of dried leaves. This is enough to induce feelings of calm and euphoria. There's a chance this could go on for six hours.

What about it causes debate?

A medical recommendation for Kratom has yet to be made due to a lack of sufficient research.

New drug development relies heavily on results from clinical trials. Research is essential for identifying potentially dangerous side effects and drug interactions. Also, the studies aid in determining safe and effective dosing ranges.

Although the effects of kratom on the body are as yet unknown, they could be profound. Almost as many alkaloids can be found in kratom as can be found in opium and magic mushrooms.

A large number of alkaloids have been shown to have powerful physiological effects on humans. However, while some of these results may be desirable, others may be cause for concern. This highlights the need for further research into this medication. There is a high potential for unwanted side effects, and its safety hasn't been proven.

One animal study indicates that mitragynine, kratom's main psychoactive alkaloid, may be addictive. Hallucinations, agitation, hyperactivity, and irritability are just some of the negative effects of dependency.

Additionally, there are no controls in place to limit kratom's production. Herbs are not subject to inspection by the Food and Drug Administration, so there is no guarantee of their quality or safety. To date, no reliable guidelines have been developed for the secure manufacture of this drug.

Affects People Have Said They Feel

Long-term kratom users may experience the following side effects.

- constipation

- loss of appetite

loss of body mass

- insomnia

• cheek discoloration

The CDC's poison control centers get a high volume of calls each year from people who have overdosed on kratom.

In conclusion

The use of kratom has been said to have positive effects. Eventually, with sufficient research, kratom may be shown to be useful. Benefits have been rumored, but no clinical evidence has been found to support them.

Without this study, many questions about this drug, such as the optimal and safe dosage, possible interactions, and harmful effects, including death, remain unanswered. Each of these factors is important to consider before choosing a medication.

CHAPTER THREE

Methods and Primers

At low doses, kratom can be stimulating, while at higher doses, it can be sedative.

In addition, it can be used to alleviate pain.

• No clinical evidence supports these applications.

Effects that could go wrong

• Dependence, loss of appetite, and sleeplessness have all been linked to long-term use.

It's possible to experience negative effects like hallucinations and loss of appetite at very low doses.

• Kratom can have fatal drug interactions with other substances and pharmaceuticals.

Can Kratom Help with Depression and Anxiety?

Factors to think about

Kratom originally grew in the tropical forests of South Asia. For a variety of ailments, including chronic pain, the leaves of the kratom tree or an extract of the leaves have been used in alternative medicine.

Self-treating symptoms of depression and anxiety with kratom is also common.

More research is needed, but there is some evidence that certain strains of kratom can help alleviate these symptoms.

The FDA has not yet given kratom the green light to treat depression or anxiety.

Because of its status as a food additive, the Food and Drug Administration has no authority over Kratom.

Take care if you're considering using kratom to alleviate symptoms of depression or anxiety.

Keep reading to learn about the supposedly positive outcomes and possible negative outcomes.

Explain how it helps with emotional states like depression and anxiety.

Although kratom isn't technically an opioid, it produces effects that are comparable to drugs like morphine and codeine.

Mitragynine is the name for kratom's active ingredient. Pain is diminished by mitragynine because it binds to opioid receptors in the brain.

Some people who use kratom report feeling less depressed and anxious as a result of this process.

The effects of kratom on mood have only recently begun to be studied.

Some people report feeling happier and less anxious after

taking kratom, which was confirmed in a 2017 study.

The sedative properties of kratom were also noted by the researchers. Its purported benefits may be nullified by side effects like sedation, which has not yet been studied.

CHAPTER FOUR

Additional Supposed Advantages

Kratom is touted as a treatment for a wide variety of ailments, not just depression and anxiety.

• pain

The Pain in Your Muscles

• fatigue

An elevated pulse rate and/or blood pressure

• Withdrawal symptoms and opioid dependence

• diarrhea

PTSD: What It Is and How to Treat It (PTSD)

Another review from 2017 found that kratom has appetite-suppressing, anti-inflammatory, and immunity-boosting properties.

Just what is kratom, then?

Thailand and Malaysia aren't the only places in Southeast Asia where you can find the kratom tree (Mitragyna speciosa).

The mitragynine, the psychoactive component of

kratom, is located in the plant's leaves.

Mitragynine is energizing at lower doses. The effects become sedative at higher doses.

Kratom has been used for medicinal purposes for hundreds of years in some regions of Southeast Asia. Kratom is also known as:

• biak

- kakum/kakuam

- ketum

- thang

- thom

The use of kratom is prohibited in many nations.

In spite of the fact that it is lawful in the USA, there have been calls for tighter control and regulation of the drug.

Is it safe for consumption, and how is it used?

Kratom can be consumed in many different ways, such as:

• capsules

• tablets

- gum

- tinctures

- extracts

Fresh or dried kratom leaves can be eaten, or the plant can be boiled into a tea.

It is also possible to ingest a powder made from dried leaves.

While smoking kratom is the more common practice, vaping it is also an option.

The effects of kratom may change depending on how it is consumed. There is currently no evidence suggesting one approach to depression and anxiety treatment is preferable over another.

CHAPTER FIVE

It's important to note that there are many distinct strains of kratom. The names given to different types of kratom typically reflect their place of origin, harvest method, or drying technique.

Like different types of marijuana, kratom can have varying degrees of influence on the user.

To date, there has been no investigation into how specifically different kratom strains work. This account is based solely on hearsay and personal experiences.

It's also important to remember that the results you get from a given strain may change depending on where you buy it.

The Maeng Da herb

The term "maeng da" is used to describe a variety of "superior" kratom strains with purportedly long-lasting effects.

While the original maeng da came from Thailand, you can also find maeng da from Indonesia and Malaysia. Maeng da comes in a variety of colors, including green, red, and white.

Claims of its stimulating effects include increased energy, improved mood, and diminished pain. After consuming maeng da, some consumers report feeling more extroverted.

Indo

The origin of Indo kratom is the Indonesian archipelago. It can appear in shades of green, red, or white.

Some types of Indo kratom may have mild energizing effects, but in general, this strain is thought to be less stimulating than others.

Indica strains from India are commonly used for their sedative effects and their ability to ease physical discomfort. Many people believe they can alleviate anxiety.

Indo-Pacific/Bali red vein

The plant that is commonly known as Bali kratom comes from that country. It has a crimson hue and is widely considered an effective painkiller.

Users have described it as having a "opioid-like" effect. Pain conditions, such as depression or chronic pain, may benefit from this.

Malay with a Green Tinge

The green variety of kratom, known as Malay kratom, is

native to that country. It has a deep emerald hue.

The drug is said to relieve pain and fatigue at low doses. It may have a more sedative effect at higher doses.

Anxiety sufferers may find relief by taking it.

Thai

Thailand is the origin of kratom. Thai kratom comes in a variety of colors, from red to green to white, and its effects may change depending on the vein color.

Strains with green and white veins are said to be stimulating and produce a pleasant "high."

Some people report feeling less pain after using red vein Thai kratom.

Borneo

The kratom used in Borneo is called Borneo kratom. There are red-veined, green-veined, and white-veined varieties.

It is widely held that Borneo kratom has a more sedative effect than other strains. It has the potential to alleviate stress and anxious feelings.

Malaysian

It is said that Malaysian strains, such as green, red, and white vein kratom, offer a happy medium between their stimulating and sedative effects.

Users have reported improvements in their mental state, decreased pain, and enhanced ability to concentrate and focus.

I was wondering if there were any recommended dosages.

The optimal kratom dosage for treating depression and anxiety is poorly understood.

The typical dosage advice takes into account factors like age, sex, and health. The effects of kratom vary not only according to dosage but also by route of administration and strain.

Kratom powder, for instance, is not nearly as effective as kratom extract.

A 2018 study based on a survey of 8,049 kratom users found that most users felt that a dose of up to 5 grams of powder taken up to 3 times a day was adequate to experience effects.

www.ingramcontent.com/pod-product-compliance
Lightning Source LLC
Chambersburg PA
CBHW070325160726
47999CB00003B/1156